TRANSFORMATIONAL TEACHING

The Art of Teaching by the Spirit

MALCOLM WEBBER

Published by:

Strategic Press
www.StrategicPress.org

Strategic Press is a division of Strategic Global Assistance, Inc.
www.sgai.org

513 S. Main St. Suite 2
Elkhart, IN 46516
U.S.A.

+1-844-532-3371 (LEADER-1)

Copyright © 2020 Malcolm Webber

ISBN: 9781888810851

All Scripture references are from the New International Version of the Bible, unless otherwise noted.

Printed in the United States of America

CONTENTS

Introduction 5

YOUR LIFE

The Purpose of Your Teaching 11
Teaching from the Indwelling Life of Christ. 15
Teaching From Him, Through Him and To Him 19
The Teacher as Leader 25
The Teacher as Intercessor. 29
The Teacher as Servant. 33
The Motive of the Teacher 41
The Two Great Commandments for the Teacher 43
The Teacher as Equipper. 47
The True Excellence of the Teacher. 51
The Sufferings of the Teacher 55
Your Time in the Word of God 61
True Teaching. 63

YOUR TEACHING

Teach Simply	69
Teach the Word of God	71
Don't "Fill the Space"	75
Don't Seek "New" Revelation	77
Always Build Up	81
Respect the Privilege of Teaching	85
The Limits of the Teacher	89
Teaching and Exhortation	93
Prepare Your Heart, Not Just Your Head	97
A Lifestyle of Preparation in the Word of God	101
Avoid the Two Extremes	105
Teach What You Know Is Real	109
Teach Soundly	111
Don't Imitate the Academics	113
Wait On God While You Teach	117
Watch God and Watch the People	123
Don't Be Afraid	125
Use the "Four Dynamics" When You Teach	127
Always Teach with Clarity, Passion and Credibility	129
Have One Point	135
Dialogue with the People You're Teaching	137
Ask Good Questions	139
Take Every Opportunity to Practice	141
Some Practical Advice	143
Protect Your Life	145
Above All Things, Live in Union with Christ	149
Final Words	151

INTRODUCTION

The teaching of the Word of God must be central to everything Christian leaders do.

These were Paul's last words to his spiritual son and successor, Timothy:

> *I charge you in the presence of God and of Christ Jesus, who is to judge the living and the dead, and by His appearing and His Kingdom: preach the Word; be ready in season and out of season; reprove, rebuke, and exhort, with complete patience and teaching. (2 Tim. 4:1-2)*

Paul's last words were, "Preach and teach the Word!" This is how important the teaching ministry is.

Significantly, teaching is the only ministry responsibility consistently mentioned in Paul's writings about requirements for church leaders (1 Tim. 3:2; 2 Tim. 2:24; Tit. 1:9).

Moreover, our teaching should be *transformational,* not only informational.

This book will describe the nature of the teaching ministry – what it means to teach the Word of God, and how you can do that effectively and in a way that brings life to God's people.

We will not focus so much on issues of biblical interpretation[1] or techniques of teaching but on the deeper issues of the life of the teacher from which his teaching proceeds.

> *Watch your life and doctrine closely. Persevere in them, because if you do, you will save both yourself and your hearers. (1 Tim. 4:16)*

Paul tells us to closely watch our lives and our teaching (not the content here but the act of teaching). First, we'll look at our lives. Then we'll give some practical advice regarding teaching ministry.

Much of what is in this book applies to every kind of spiritual leadership and ministry.

---

1 Please see *What Does the Bible Say?* by Malcolm Webber for an extensive study of biblical interpretation.

Our goals and hopes by the end of this book are that you:

- Are inspired by the reality of your own God-given calling to teach deeply and effectively.
- Have a clear and biblically-sound understanding of how a Christian leader should teach.
- Make immediate practical applications to improve your own teaching.
- Have been refreshed, encouraged, empowered and motivated in your life and teaching ministry.
- Have an increased desire and capacity to be a healthy leader who will teach well and lead God's people into His fullness.

Finally, this book has 40 chapters. Each chapter is a somewhat independent thought. Prayerfully read one chapter per day. In 40 days your teaching ministry will greatly improve.

Malcolm Webber, Ph.D.
March 2020

YOUR LIFE

THE PURPOSE OF YOUR TEACHING

Why do you teach? What is your purpose?

Paul and John were very clear about their purpose in teaching:

> *[Christ] we proclaim, warning everyone and teaching everyone with all wisdom, that we may present everyone mature in Christ. (Col. 1:28)*

> *All Scripture is breathed out by God and profitable for teaching, for reproof, for correction, and for training in righteousness, that the man of God may be complete, equipped for every good work. (2 Tim. 3:16-17)*

> *That which was from the beginning, which we have heard, which we have seen with our eyes, which we looked upon and have touched with our hands, concerning the Word*

> *of life – the life was made manifest, and we have seen it, and testify to it and proclaim to you the eternal life, which was with the Father and was made manifest to us – that which we have seen and heard we proclaim also to you, so that you too may have fellowship with us; and indeed our fellowship is with the Father and with His Son Jesus Christ. (1 John 1:1-3)*
>
> *And we know that the Son of God has come and has given us understanding, so that we may know Him who is true; and we are in Him who is true, in His Son Jesus Christ. He is the true God and eternal life. (1 John 5:20)*

What was their ultimate purpose in teaching the Word of God?

Clearly, it was to bring people to Christ – to deep union with Him – that they might know Him; then from His indwelling life, their lives might be completely changed and brought to maturity.

Thus, your purpose in teaching must always be *life transformation*.

Your purpose must not be:

- Purely intellectual and informational
- Entertainment
- To receive payment
- To share your opinions on political or social issues
- To perpetuate human traditions

- To cover content and complete a course
- To show off your biblical knowledge or teaching skill
- To gain a personal following
- Competition with other leaders or teachers
- To "fill a spot" on Sunday morning
- Just doing it because we've always done it in the past

The proof of your teaching ministry is the changed lives of the people you serve.

> *... on the day of our Lord Jesus you will boast of us as we will boast of you. (2 Cor. 1:14)*

> *Therefore, my brothers, whom I love and long for, my joy and crown, stand firm thus in the Lord, my beloved. (Phil. 4:1)*

> *For what is our hope or joy or crown of boasting before our Lord Jesus at His coming? Is it not you? For you are our glory and joy. (1 Thess. 2:19-20)*

Pause and assess your past and current motivations as a teacher. Are any of them impure? Confess these to God and ask Him to align your heart to His.

TEACHING FROM THE INDWELLING LIFE OF CHRIST

When Jesus taught, He continually looked at His Father. He lived in continuous fellowship with His Father. This inward, spiritual fellowship was the source of everything in His life and ministry – including His teaching.

> *... My teaching is not My own. It comes from the One who sent Me. (John 7:16)*

> *... I do nothing on My own but speak just what the Father has taught Me. (John 8:28)*

> *... the Son can do nothing by Himself; He can do only what He sees His Father doing ... (John 5:19)*

> *By Myself I can do nothing; I judge only as I hear ... (John 5:30)*

Inwardly, Jesus listened to God, waited on God, relied on God. He did not merely teach out of His own understanding.

Thus, Jesus revealed not simply His own life but the life and Person of His Father to the world:

> *If you really knew Me, you would know My Father as well. From now on, you do know Him and have seen Him ... Anyone who has seen Me has seen the Father ... (John 14:7-9)*

In the relationship between Jesus and His Father, we find a parallel to what our own relationship with God can be.

> *Whoever eats My flesh and drinks My blood abides in Me, and I in him. Just as the living Father sent Me and I live because of the Father, so the one who feeds on Me will live because of Me. (John 6:56-57)*

> *... He who loves Me will be loved by My Father, and I too will love him and show myself to him ... My Father will love him, and We will come to him and make Our home with him. (John 14:21-23)*

> *But when He, the Spirit of truth, comes, He will guide you into all truth. He will not speak on His own; He*

> *will speak only what He hears, and He will tell you what is yet to come. He will bring glory to Me by taking from what is Mine and making it known to you. All that belongs to the Father is Mine. That is why I said the Spirit will take from what is Mine and make it known to you. (John 16:13-15)*

Jesus looked at the Father and listened to His voice and thus perfectly revealed Him to the world. The Holy Spirit now looks at the Son and listens to Him and thus reveals the Son of God to us. We are then to reveal His life to others.

This revelation – this expression of the nature and being of God – is the nature of our teaching.

As this divine fellowship was the source of Jesus' teaching, so your experience of divine fellowship will be the source of your teaching.

> *But we all, with unveiled face, beholding as in a mirror the glory of the Lord, are being transformed into the same image from glory to glory, just as by the Spirit of the Lord. (2 Cor. 3:18, NKJV)*

> *… If a man abides in Me and I in him, he will bear much fruit; apart from Me you can do nothing. (John 15:5)*

This is the simple nature of true Christian teaching: union with Jesus, and teaching from His indwelling life.

This means that to the extent you are living in union with Christ you will have life and power in your teaching. If your teaching is not changing people's lives, then your solution is not just to study harder and learn more. Your solution is not just to learn new teaching techniques or incorporate technology into your presentations. Your solution is to find God more deeply – to know Him, to love Him. When you experience His life, you will have life for others. *The fruit of your outward ministry will never exceed the depth of your inward life in Christ.*

TEACHING FROM HIM, THROUGH HIM AND TO HIM

> *... from Him and through Him and to Him are all things ... (Rom. 11:36)*

This is a beautiful three-part framework to help us think about healthy teaching ministry. The true ministry of teaching is not the same kind of teaching that you received at school. It's profoundly different – in origin, practice and results.

Our teaching must be *from* Him. It must proceed from His indwelling life.

Our teaching must be *through* Him. As we teach, we listen to Him, love Him, and then express His will, His purpose, His life to His people.

Our teaching must be *to* Him. The purpose of our teaching is to change lives and to fulfill God's will and glorify Him.

What are the opposites of each?

	Two Kinds of Teaching		
	Origin	**Practice**	**Results**
Healthy Teaching	From Him: It must proceed from His indwelling life.	Through Him: As we teach, we listen to Him, love Him, and then express His will, His purpose, His life to His people.	To Him: The purpose of our teaching is to change lives and to fulfill God's will and glorify Him.
Unhealthy Teaching	Our teaching is from our own human learning.	As we teach, we trust in our own learning and ability.	The purpose of our teaching is to show off our own knowledge and to bring the people into outward conformity and under our control.

The religious leaders of Jesus' day exemplified unhealthy teaching.

> *And they reviled him, saying, "You are His disciple, but we are disciples of Moses. We know that God has spoken to Moses, but as for this man, we do not know where He comes from." (John 9:28-29)*
>
> *They answered him, "You were born in utter sin, and would you teach us?" And they cast him out. (John 9:34)*

Their work did not come from their relationship with God. As a result, they were insecure and competitive. They relied on their own knowledge. They were intimidating and manipulative. They were self-serving, proud and arrogant. "We are disciples of Moses!" "Would you teach us?"

Look at Jesus' interaction with them in John 7:

> *About the middle of the feast Jesus went up into the temple and began teaching. The Jews therefore marveled, saying, "How is it that this man has learning, when He has never studied?" So Jesus answered them, "My teaching is not Mine, but His who sent Me. If anyone's will is to do God's will, he will know whether the teaching is from God or whether I am speaking on My own authority. The one who speaks on his own authority seeks his own glory; but the One who seeks the glory of Him who sent Him is true, and in Him there is no falsehood. (John 7:14-18)*

The Jewish leaders recognized that Jesus' teaching was very different from their own.

What were the differences?

	Two Kinds of Teaching		
	Origin	Practice	Results
Jesus' Teaching	The eternal life and wisdom of God	Out of the indwelling life of the Father By the power of the Holy Spirit With divine authority	The glory of the Father Life change for the hearers
Religious Leaders' Teaching	Their own learning Human tradition	By their own ability With human logic and arguments With human authority	Their own glory External conformity by the hearers Heavy burdens on the people

Jesus sternly rebuked them:

> ... *His voice you have never heard, His form you have never seen, and you do not have His Word abiding in you, for you do not believe the One whom He has sent. You search the Scriptures because you think that in them you have eternal life; and it is they that bear witness about Me, yet you refuse to come to Me that you may have life. (John 5:37-40)*

Don't follow their example. Be a healthy teacher!

THE TEACHER AS LEADER

Teaching should *never* be only for the purpose of sharing information.[2]

Teaching is an act of leadership.

Leadership means *movement*.[3] The leader helps people move to a better place in the purposes of God.

Therefore, your teaching must *always* lead to action and to life change – to movement – or else it's the wrong kind of teaching!

---

[2] Sadly, the model for many Christian teachers was their years of education at school. That's where they learned what "teaching" is and they do it the same way. However, teaching the Word of God is quite distinct from school teaching, as we will see. It's a different paradigm.

[3] For more on this please see *Leadership: SpiritBuilt Leadership 1* by Malcolm Webber.

This requires clarity on the part of the teacher. You must ask yourself: what is my specific transformational goal in this teaching?

Your goal must *never* be that the people merely "understand" something. Your goal must be life change. Your goal must be movement. Of course, that includes understanding, but it must not be limited to that.

What do you hope that the people will do after your teaching? Is there even anything they could possibly do? Sadly, many teachings do not have any clear calls to action – their academic and theoretical nature precludes the possibility of active responses other than "agreeing" or "knowing."[4]

Agreement by itself is not the path to change. Obedience is the path to change.

> *But be doers of the Word, and not hearers only, deceiving yourselves. For if anyone is a hearer of the Word and not a doer, he is like a man who looks intently at his natural face in a mirror. For he looks at himself and goes away and at once forgets what he was like. But the one who looks into the perfect law, the law of liberty, and perseveres, being no hearer who forgets but a doer who acts, he will be blessed in his doing. (Jam. 1:22-25)*

The teacher is a leader and must teach like one!

---

4 Please see Malcolm Webber's model, "The Four Dynamics of Transformation." The third dynamic is the experiential dynamic – the power of action.

There are three parts to leadership:[5]

1. The leader establishes the direction.
2. He aligns the people in that direction.
3. He motivates and inspires them to move and keep moving in that direction until they fulfill the vision.

Your teaching must connect with all three parts. To help people move, your teaching must clearly share the vision, bring deep ownership of the people for that vision and help them to move in the direction of the vision. This is the power of teaching.

Leadership is movement. Teaching must create movement!

---

[5] For more on this please see *Leading: SpiritBuilt Leadership 3* by Malcolm Webber.

THE TEACHER AS INTERCESSOR

Your teaching must be in the power of the Spirit. In the New Testament, teaching was *always* energized by the Holy Spirit.

> *And Jesus returned in the power of the Spirit to Galilee, and a report about Him went out through all the surrounding country. And He taught in their synagogues, being glorified by all. (Luke 4:14-15)*

After 40 days of prayer and fasting, Jesus taught "in the power of the Spirit."

> *… our Gospel came to you not only in word, but also in power and in the Holy Spirit and with full conviction … (1 Thess. 1:5)*

Intercession releases the spiritual power to bring deep change. Thus, Paul's teaching was deeply connected to his intercession for those whom he served.

> [Christ] we proclaim, warning everyone and teaching everyone with all wisdom, that we may present everyone mature in Christ. For this also I toil, struggling with all His energy that He powerfully works within me. For I want you to know how great a struggle I have for you and for those at Laodicea and for all who have not seen me face to face, that their hearts may be encouraged, being knit together in love, to reach all the riches of full assurance of understanding and the knowledge of God's mystery, which is Christ, in whom are hidden all the treasures of wisdom and knowledge. (Col. 1:28 – 2:3, Greek)

In Colossians 1:28 Paul refers to his ministry:

> [Christ] we proclaim, warning everyone and teaching everyone with all wisdom, that we may present everyone mature in Christ.

His purpose was to lead the people to maturity in Christ. To achieve this purpose, Paul did two things. First, he taught. Then, the next verse in the Greek text says that he *also* "struggled" toward this goal. Moreover, he struggled "with all God's energy." The Greek word for "struggle" is the root of the modern English word, "agonize."

> *For this I also toil, struggling with all His energy that He powerfully works within me. (Col. 1:29, Greek)*

Clearly this refers to Paul's intercession on their behalf. The following verses in the early part of Chapter 2 describe how Paul did this for people he had never met so it cannot refer to any kind of direct personal ministry.

> *For I want you to know how great a struggle I have for you and for those at Laodicea and for all who have not seen me face to face, that their hearts may be encouraged, being knit together in love, to reach all the riches of full assurance of understanding and the knowledge of God's mystery, which is Christ … (Col. 2:1-2)*

This is why Paul's ministry was so deep and so impactful. This is why he was able to teach with such power and deep conviction (1 Cor. 2:1-5; 1 Thess. 1:5).

Thus, it is not enough for a leader merely to teach and preach; he must also travail in prayer for those to whom he ministers.

Moreover, this is not some quick "Lord please bless the people" prayer. Paul struggled in prayer "with all His energy that He powerfully works within me"! This was deep union with Christ in His burden and passion for the people.

Later in the book, Paul speaks of Epaphras' deep intercession for the Colossians and others:

> *Epaphras, who is one of you, a servant of Christ Jesus, greets you, always struggling on your behalf in his prayers, that you may stand mature and fully assured in all the will of God. For I bear him witness that he has worked hard for you and for those in Laodicea and in Hierapolis. (Col. 4:12-13)*

We also see Paul's deep travail for the saints in Galatia who were in deception:

> *My little children, of whom I travail in birth again until Christ be formed in you ... (Gal. 4:19, KJV; cf. John 11:33, 35, 38; Rom. 8:26-27)*

There is no shortcut to powerful teaching. It does not come merely from accurate knowledge and the mastery of mechanical teaching techniques. Powerful teaching comes from intercession.

To be truly effective, teachers must be intercessors.

THE TEACHER AS SERVANT

Then the mother of the sons of Zebedee came up to Him with her sons, and kneeling before Him she asked Him for something. And He said to her, "What do you want?" She said to Him, "Say that these two sons of mine are to sit, one at Your right hand and one at Your left, in Your Kingdom." Jesus answered, "You do not know what you are asking. Are you able to drink the cup that I am to drink?" They said to Him, "We are able." He said to them, "You will drink My cup, but to sit at My right hand and at My left is not Mine to grant, but it is for those for whom it has been prepared by My Father."

And when the ten heard it, they were indignant at the two brothers. But Jesus called them to Him and said,

> "You know that the rulers of the Gentiles lord it over them, and their great ones exercise authority over them. It shall not be so among you. But whoever would be great among you must be your servant, and whoever would be first among you must be your slave, even as the Son of Man came not to be served but to serve, and to give His life as a ransom for many." (Matt. 20:20-28)

This was Jesus' greatest teaching on servanthood.

He was responding to the request of the mother of James and John. She asked for power and authority. In response, Jesus asked, "Are you able to drink the cup (of suffering) that I am to drink?" In dramatic contrast to the world's pursuit of greatness that is taken by force, Jesus showed us that the only path to glory is the way of the Cross – the path of rejection and pain.

Then He went right to the heart of the matter. The true leader is not a "ruler" as the world thinks; rather, he is a servant.

The essence of "abusiveness" in leadership is using followers for the leader's own interests.

> ... Woe to the shepherds of Israel who only take care of themselves! Should not shepherds take care of the flock? You eat the curds, clothe yourselves with the wool and slaughter the choice animals, but you do not take care of the flock. You have not strengthened the weak or healed the sick or bound up the injured. You

> *have not brought back the strays or searched for the lost. You have ruled them harshly and brutally. So they were scattered because there was no shepherd ... My flock lacks a shepherd and so has been plundered and has become food for all the wild animals, and because My shepherds did not search for My flock but cared for themselves rather than for My flock ... (Ezek. 34:2-8)*

> *I have no one else like him [i.e. Timothy], who takes a genuine interest in your welfare. For everyone looks out for his own interests, not those of Jesus Christ. (Phil. 2:20-21; cf. John 10:12-13; Acts 20:29-31; Rom. 16:18; 2 Cor. 11:20; Phil. 1:17; 2 Pet. 2:3)*

In contrast, the essence of servant leadership is seeking what is best for the followers in the purposes of God, and not oneself.

> *... the Son of Man did not come to be served, but to serve, and to give His life as a ransom for many. (Mark 10:45)*

> *Even as I please all men in all things, not seeking mine own profit, but the profit of many, that they may be saved. (1 Cor. 10:33; cf. 4:5, 15; 12:14-15, 17-19; Phil. 1:7-8, 25-26; 2:17; 1 Thess. 3:8; 1 Pet. 5:1-4)*

The true teacher of God's Word is a servant to the people. His primary motivation is what is best for the people, and not himself. He does not use the people. He does not pursue status, prestige, comfort, security or financial gain. He does not teach to display his own knowledge or speaking skill. He pursues the good of the people.

He serves them with humility and love. He serves them with tenderness and compassion. He teaches them with brokenness of heart and tears when necessary. He genuinely seeks what is best for them.[6]

Even when addressing "opponents" the teacher must treat them with patience, hope and gentleness:

> *Have nothing to do with foolish, ignorant controversies; you know that they breed quarrels. And the Lord's servant must not be quarrelsome but kind to everyone, able to teach, patiently enduring evil, correcting his opponents with gentleness. God may perhaps grant them repentance leading to a knowledge of the truth, and they may come to their senses and escape from the snare of the devil, after being captured by him to do his will. (2 Tim. 2:23-26)*

This is the way of the true teaching ministry. It is the path of self-giving love – not because the teacher has to, but because he wants to; because he genuinely loves God's people and longs for them with the affection of Jesus Christ.

This is the teacher whom God will honor!

---

[6] The two characteristics of "legitimate vision" are that it's from God (not you) and that it serves others (not yourself).

> *Let each of you look not only to his own interests, but also to the interests of others. Have this mind among yourselves, which is yours in Christ Jesus, who, though He was in the form of God, did not count equality with God a thing to be grasped, but emptied Himself, by taking the form of a servant, being born in the likeness of men. And being found in human form, He humbled Himself by becoming obedient to the point of death, even death on a Cross. Therefore God has highly exalted Him and bestowed on Him the Name that is above every name ... (Phil. 2:4-9)*

In contrast, look at the motives of the Pharisees:

> *They do all their deeds to be seen by others. For they make their phylacteries broad and their fringes long, and they love the place of honor at feasts and the best seats in the synagogues and greetings in the marketplaces and being called rabbi by others. (Matt. 23:5-7)*

In the lives of the Pharisees we see that everything in their leadership and in their teaching revolved around themselves. They saw themselves as the masters of the people and they loved it. They loved the feeling of power. They loved the idea that they had superior knowledge. They loved the respect and admiration they received.

As we saw in a previous section, the Pharisees' pride was dramatically revealed in John 9 when they interacted with the blind man Jesus had healed:

"You are His disciple, but we are disciples of Moses."
(v. 28)

"You were born in utter sin, and would you teach us?"
(v. 34)

They had such pride and superiority. "We are Moses' disciples. How dare you lecture us! Don't you know who we are?"

To be a healthy teacher and to see lives changed, you must stay small in your own eyes. Don't take yourself too seriously.

The Pharisees had human authority but they had no divine authority or power. Even though they taught the Scriptures, they were completely separated from God and their ministry was death to people.

You must be honest in your heart before God. You must continually open your heart to God: "Lord, test me, try me." And if you ever hear yourself thinking toward someone else, "Who are you to lecture me?" then be afraid. Stop and get down before God and ask Him to deal deeply with your heart.

Jesus was God. He actually was superior – vastly superior. Yet He came as a servant. He preferred us. He left behind the glory, privilege and honor of the throne of God and came to serve us. He chose our good over His own and because of that, God exalted Him as highest of all.

If you desire true spiritual authority in your teaching it will only be because you have first gone very low, deeply embracing servanthood and genuinely putting the good of the people before your own.

The people belong to God. They do not belong to you. It's not your right to treat them however you want. It's not your right to use them for your own exaltation. One day, we will all give an account for our lives and ministries. We will stand before God and He will ask us, "How did you treat my precious sons and daughters?"

So, treat God's people with gentleness, with care and with self-giving love – not harshness or intimidation. Don't use them for your own pride or exaltation.

If you stay small in your own eyes, then God can give you true authority in your teaching.

Amazingly, right at the end of His stern words in Matthew 23, Jesus anguished over the very people He had just rebuked!

> "O Jerusalem, Jerusalem, the city that kills the prophets and stones those who are sent to it! How often would I have gathered your children together as a hen gathers her brood under her wings, and you were not willing! See, your house is left to you desolate. For I tell you, you will not see Me again, until you say, 'Blessed is He who comes in the name of the Lord.'" (Matt. 23:37-39)

Even when Jesus dealt so severely with the wicked Pharisees, we still see His affection, His love, and His commitment to His people. How much more should you love and serve the people for whom Jesus died?

THE MOTIVE OF THE TEACHER

Teachers are given the extraordinary privilege of being in the middle of a magnificent interaction between God and His people! It's not about you; it's about Him and them.

Your goal is not to impress people with your knowledge.

> *For what we proclaim is not ourselves, but Jesus Christ as Lord, with ourselves as your servants for Jesus' sake. (2 Cor. 4:5)*

Therefore, don't teach complicated things that few people understand. Teach in a way that everyone listening can follow.

God wants all His people to know the Truth, not only an elite few!

> *Him we proclaim, warning everyone and teaching everyone with all wisdom, that we may present everyone mature in Christ. (Col. 1:28)*

Stop trying to impress people. Your goal is not that people say at the end, "What a great message that was!" or "What a great teacher!"

Neither is your goal to prove to everyone that you're as good, or better, than other teachers. It's not a competition.

Your goal is that the lives of the people are changed. Be honest with yourself and your motives.

THE TWO GREAT COMMANDMENTS FOR THE TEACHER

Jesus said there are two great commandments:

> *And one of them, a lawyer, asked Him a question to test Him. "Teacher, which is the great commandment in the Law?" And He said to him, "You shall love the Lord your God with all your heart and with all your soul and with all your mind. This is the great and first commandment. And a second is like it: You shall love your neighbor as yourself. On these two commandments depend all the Law and the Prophets." (Matt. 22:35-40)*

Jesus taught these two commandments in response to the attempt by the Pharisees to trick Him. In these two commandments there is a clear rebuke to them.

Their teaching and ministry was not out of love for God. They loved themselves, their own tradition, their own comfort, their own honor.

And they did not love the people. They used the people and exploited them.

Let your teaching ministry be different!

Paul shows us the centrality of love in everything we do:

> *If I speak in the tongues of men and of angels, but have not love, I am a noisy gong or a clanging cymbal. And if I have prophetic powers, and understand all mysteries and all knowledge, and if I have all faith, so as to remove mountains, but have not love, I am nothing. If I give away all I have, and if I deliver up my body to be burned, but have not love, I gain nothing. (1 Cor. 13:1-3)*

The teacher must have a heart of love for God's people (Matt. 22:35-40). This is what must motivate you – deep commitment to His Bride.

If you are motivated by love, then your knowledge of the Word and your skill in speaking will be a great blessing to others.

But if you lack this motivation, and all you have is knowledge and preaching skills, your ministry will be empty. You won't be a blessing to others. You will get burned out. You will end up proud because of your superior knowledge, but not pleasing to either God or man.

Of course, you should grow in knowledge of the Word and be an excellent communicator, but you must do it from love. Then you will minister life.

Paul's letters are filled with his tenderness and compassion toward the people:

> *… we were gentle among you, like a nursing mother taking care of her own children. So, being affectionately desirous of you, we were ready to share with you not only the Gospel of God but also our own selves, because you had become very dear to us. (1 Thess. 2:7-8)*

> *… my little children, for whom I am again in the anguish of childbirth until Christ is formed in you! (Gal. 4:19)*

> *For God is my witness, how I yearn for you all with the affection of Christ Jesus. (Phil. 1:8)*

> *Therefore, my brothers, whom I love and long for, my joy and crown, stand firm thus in the Lord, my beloved. (Phil. 4:1)*

Paul's love for the people was not based upon their deserving it. They were not perfect. Often the same letters that expressed such deep affection contained serious corrections. He loved them with the unconditional love of the Father.

Without this love – this self-giving and affectionate love – your teaching will just be a noisy gong or a clanging symbol (1 Cor. 13:1).

THE TEACHER AS EQUIPPER

In Ephesians 4:12, Paul says that a primary role of the teacher, as well as the other ministries, is to equip the people to function properly in the life of the Church.

> *And He gave the apostles, the prophets, the evangelists, the shepherds and teachers, to equip the saints for the work of ministry, for building up the Body of Christ ... (Eph. 4:11-12)*

These five kinds of ministries are to equip the people so they do the work of the ministry which, in turn, will build up the Body of Christ to maturity.

Thus, the role of the teacher is not only to teach the people the Word of God. It is also – and primarily – to equip the people to study and know the Word of God for themselves.

This does not reduce the authority of the teacher. Paul was not threatened when the Bereans studied the Word for themselves and did not simply believe his teaching without question.

> *Now these Jews [at Berea] were more noble than those in Thessalonica; they received the Word with all eagerness, examining the Scriptures daily to see if these things were so. (Acts 17:11)*

Paul would have loved this! Luke described the Bereans as "more noble" because they took responsibility themselves to study and accurately know the Word.

Jesus Himself also expected that the people to whom He was preaching had read the Word of God, and that they knew what it meant (e.g., Matt. 12:3-5; 19:4; 21:42; 22:31)!

> *[Jesus] said to him, "What is written in the Law? How do you read it?" And he answered, "You shall love the Lord your God with all your heart and with all your soul and with all your strength and with all your mind, and your neighbor as yourself." And He said to him, "You have answered correctly; do this, and you will live." (Luke 10:26-28)*

Jesus expected the man to know, and then Jesus affirmed that there was a "correct" answer.

It was the desire and hope of the New Testament leaders that the people of God love the Word of God and deeply know the Word for themselves:

> *For though by this time you ought to be teachers, you need someone to teach you again the basic principles of the oracles of God ... (Heb. 5:12)*
>
> *Let the Word of Christ dwell in you richly, teaching and admonishing one another in all wisdom ... (Col. 3:16)*
>
> *... and what you have heard from me in the presence of many witnesses entrust to faithful men, who will be able to teach others also. (2 Tim. 2:2)*

This is a profound distinction and it changes how the teacher must teach. Too often, teachers enjoy the dependency of the people upon them – the teacher is recognized as the one who knows the Word and the people all look to him. That must change.

The teacher must nurture two things:

- A passionate *vision* within the people for the importance, centrality and power of the Word of God, so that they love the Word, want to study the Word, and obey the Word.

- The *capacity* to study the Word well, interpret it properly, apply it soundly to their lives, and then teach others.

The healthy teacher is not merely the "expert" whom everyone else looks to and depends on. The healthy teacher is, instead, an equipper who nurtures a culture in which everyone is building others:

- Parents are responsible to build their children (Eph. 6:4; Deut. 6:4-9; 11:18-21).
- Existing believers are responsible to build the new disciples (Matt. 28:19-20).
- The older women are responsible to build the younger ones (Tit. 2:3-5).
- The mature men should teach the younger men (2 Tim. 2:2).
- Leaders must build leaders (Mark 3:14).
- We are always to take every opportunity to build one another's lives (Rom. 15:2; 1 Cor. 14:26).

THE TRUE EXCELLENCE OF THE TEACHER

In John 9, Jesus healed a man who had been blind from birth. This upset the religious leaders and they angrily questioned the man who had been healed.

> *So for the second time they called the man who had been blind and said to him, "Give glory to God. We know that this man is a sinner." He answered, "Whether He is a sinner I do not know. One thing I do know, that though I was blind, now I see."*
>
> *They said to him, "What did He do to you? How did He open your eyes?" He answered them, "I have told you already, and you would not listen. Why do you*

want to hear it again? Do you also want to become His disciples?" And they reviled him, saying, "You are His disciple, but we are disciples of Moses. We know that God has spoken to Moses, but as for this man, we do not know where He comes from."

The man answered, "Why, this is an amazing thing! You do not know where He comes from, and yet He opened my eyes. We know that God does not listen to sinners, but if anyone is a worshiper of God and does His will, God listens to him. Never since the world began has it been heard that anyone opened the eyes of a man born blind. If this man were not from God, He could do nothing."

They answered him, "You were born in utter sin, and would you teach us?" And they cast him out. (John 9:24-34)

In this exchange we see the deep pride of the religious leaders:

"You are His disciple, but we are disciples of Moses." (v. 28)

"You were born in utter sin, and would you teach us?" (v. 34)

The religious leaders were proud of their learning, of their teacher (cf. 1 Cor. 3:4), and of their mastery of knowledge. They thought they were excellent in every way. But Jesus called them "blind" (vv. 39-41).

The more that you know and the greater that your teachers have been, the more you will be tempted by this same pride. You must beware of this. If you ever hear yourself thinking toward someone else, "Who are you to teach me?" you must quickly repent!

Thus, your excellence as a teacher is not a matter of how much you know or who you learned it from. Your excellence is in your humility, your servanthood, your union with Christ and your love for His people.

THE SUFFERINGS OF THE TEACHER

In 2 Corinthians, Paul profoundly connected the ministry of the teacher with the suffering of the teacher:

> *For God, who said, "Let light shine out of darkness," has shone in our hearts to give the light of the knowledge of the glory of God in the face of Jesus Christ. But we have this treasure in jars of clay, to show that the surpassing power belongs to God and not to us. We are afflicted in every way, but not crushed; perplexed, but not driven to despair; persecuted, but not forsaken; struck down, but not destroyed; always carrying in the body the death of Jesus, so that the life of Jesus may also be manifested in our bodies. For we who live are always being given over to death for Jesus' sake, so that the life of Jesus also may be manifested in our*

> *mortal flesh. So death is at work in us, but life in you.*
> *(2 Cor. 4:6-12)*

We have beautiful "treasure" in our lives. The treasure is Him, His Presence, His glory, His Truth, His life. But this treasure is in weak "jars of clay" and God allows these jars of clay to be broken – "afflicted," "perplexed," "persecuted," "dying." God continually allows the jars to break to show that the "surpassing power belongs to God and not to us" – so that others may see the treasure inside.

Thus, to the extent that suffering and "death" works in you is the extent to which you will have "life" for others.

Why is this so? Paul tells us in the first chapter:

> *For we do not want you to be unaware, brothers, of the affliction we experienced in Asia. For we were so utterly burdened beyond our strength that we despaired of life itself. Indeed, we felt that we had received the sentence of death. But that was to make us rely not on ourselves but on God who raises the dead. (2 Cor. 1:8-9)*

God allows you to go through sufferings that are "beyond your strength" so that you turn deeply to Him. When you turn to Him in surrender and dependency then you will find His love, His grace, His Presence, His Truth – and then you will have life for others.

This is the price the teacher must pay to have life for others. Are you willing to pay this price?

If you want to have life for others – if you want to give eternal treasure to others – then this is the path. This is the life of the teacher and this is the spiritual reality of the teaching ministry. It's not just about scholarship and learning, and working hard to be a great communicator. It's not trying to make the jar beautiful. Real teaching is about brokenness. Real teaching comes from union with Christ – in His death and in His life. This is when you will have life for others, when they will see treasure, when the excellency is of Him and not of you.

Are you willing to pay this price?

We're all different. We're all jars of clay, but we're all different kinds of jars. That means the way God deals with each of us is different, and the kinds of suffering that God allows us to go through is different for each of us. For some, that will involve a severe persecution of their faith. For others, it might be rejection. For someone else, it may be various kinds of pressure and stress. For others, it's the pain of church-life. For some, it might be physical sickness or financial pressure or loss. For others, it might be family issues – marriage trouble or children who are not walking with God.

Your life will not look like somebody else's. The brokenness God allows to come to you will not be the same as somebody else's. But the purpose is the same – and the love of God that is behind it is the same. Moreover, the vision of God that you will be a carrier of His treasure is the same, and the faithfulness of God to you in the midst of the fire is the same.

In His love, even though God allows continual breaking, you will not be crushed. God allows you to be broken but He does not destroy you.

Therefore, your response to God in the midst of the fire must be the same as Paul's response was. You must turn away from your own excellence, from trusting in your own wisdom, knowledge and strength. Turn your heart fully to Him and embrace union with Him in His Cross. Look more purely at His face. Surrender more deeply to Him and His will. That's why He allows it.

God does not allow suffering because He's angry with you or because you have failed in some way, but because His eternal purpose is upon your life. He wants you to have His treasure to give to others. He wants you to have life – not just theory and human techniques. This is the meaning of your suffering and the purpose of your pain.

In the end, it's not about you at all – it's about Him, and it's about those He wants to touch. He wants them to know His treasure. He wants them to see His glory. He wants them to have His life. This is why He gives you the privilege of carrying this treasure in a jar of clay that He allows to break. You have the extraordinary privilege and honor of giving His treasure to others. Death is at work in you but life is at work in those you serve.

> *For it is all for your sake, so that as grace extends to more and more people it may increase thanksgiving, to the glory of God. (2 Cor. 4:15)*

Embrace your calling to brokenness, knowing that God will not allow you to be destroyed, and knowing that your suffering – however bad it seems at the time – is only light and momentary!

> *So we do not lose heart. Though our outer self is wasting away, our inner self is being renewed day by day. For this light momentary affliction is preparing for us an eternal weight of glory beyond all comparison, as we look not to the things that are seen but to the things that are unseen. For the things that are seen are transient, but the things that are unseen are eternal. (2 Cor. 4:16-18)*

Your suffering "is preparing ... an eternal weight of glory"! It is bringing forth a great harvest – a harvest of life in Christ, of truth, of treasure. It's a harvest of the Presence and glory of God. This is the meaning of your suffering. So, don't give up. Don't back out of the fight. Stay in the race. Give yourself to God. Embrace His purposes whether you understand them or not.

You don't have to understand everything He does. He understands it all perfectly! He's not asking you to figure it out. He's asking you to trust Him, to love Him, to surrender to Him, to follow Him and to never give up.

Therefore, you can walk boldly into the future God has prepared for you knowing that whatever He allows comes from His hand of love. He will be faithful to you. You will stand before Him one day soon before His glorious throne and there will be multitudes who are there because of your life, your faith, and your willingness to pay the price to embrace the shattering of the jar to give the treasure to them.

In the end, it is all for His glorious, beautiful Bride. That is why you labor. That is why you suffer. That is why you must not give up.

YOUR TIME IN THE WORD OF GOD

If you are going to have life when you teach, you must begin the practice of spending time in the Word of God *only* for your own nourishment.

Spend time in the Word *only* to find God for yourself – to know Him, to see Him, to love Him. Do not spend time in the Word to prepare to give a teaching to someone else.

Don't be worried that if you do this, then your preparation to teach others will suffer. If you are personally finding God deeply in His Word, then you'll have more than enough to teach to others when you need to. It will be there and it will be alive.

Preparation is absolutely necessary but it must be the right kind of preparation – not just intellectual study but deep and living engagement with God.

The Bible is not just a textbook that you need to teach to others. It is the primary source of life for your own life!

Certainly this includes diligent study but it also includes meditation in the Word, reflection before the Holy Spirit, praying the Word, responding to the Word, and simply reading the Word with no ministry agenda in mind.

The depth and fruit of your teaching ministry will come directly from the quality of your life in God.

Before He began His ministry, Jesus spent 40 days in the wilderness. He was not doing academic study during that time. He was praying, fasting and communing with His Father. Then He "returned in the power of the Spirit" (Luke 4:14) and began His work.

Let your ministry also come directly from the reality of your life in God!

TRUE TEACHING

Today, many people call themselves "Christian teachers" but they do not all have the gift of teaching.

In Ephesians and Romans, Paul speaks about the "gift" of teaching:

> *… He gave gifts to men … And He gave the apostles, the prophets, the evangelists, the shepherds and teachers … (Eph. 4:8-11)*

> *Having gifts that differ according to the grace given to us, let us use them: if prophecy, in proportion to our faith; if service, in our serving; the one who teaches, in his teaching; (Rom. 12:6-7)*

The true gift of teaching is not merely a natural human ability, and it does not function the way that the ability of a college professor, for example, does.

There are two aspects to the gift of teaching:

- Deep insight into the Word. This does not mean the revelation of "new" things but spiritual insight into the "old" truths of the Scriptures so that they become life to you.
- Impartation. The teacher gives spiritual life, not merely intellectual information.

Both of these are the work of the Holy Spirit.

First, the Holy Spirit reveals God's Truth to us. It is not simply the result of human effort and understanding.

> *… these things God has revealed to us through the Spirit. For the Spirit searches everything, even the depths of God … Now we have received not the spirit of the world, but the Spirit who is from God, that we might understand the things freely given us by God. (1 Cor. 2:10-12)*

Second, by the Holy Spirit, we teach those truths to others:

> *And we impart this in words not taught by human wisdom but taught by the Spirit, interpreting spiritual truths to those who are spiritual. (1 Cor. 2:13)*

Thus, at the heart of the true ministry of teaching is a deep connection to, and reliance upon, the Holy Spirit. This stands in marked contrast to the teaching of the world which relies entirely upon one's own learning and ability.

Thus, the true teacher receives life from God and then gives that life to others. By the Spirit, the Word changes you and then, by the Spirit, the Word changes others.

This is beyond the realm of intellectual information. The true gift of teaching changes lives.

> *For I long to see you, that I may impart to you some spiritual gift to strengthen you ... (Rom. 1:11)*
>
> *I know that when I come to you I will come in the fullness of the blessing of Christ. (Rom. 15:29)*
>
> *... our Gospel came to you not only in word, but also in power and in the Holy Spirit and with full conviction ... (1 Thess. 1:5)*
>
> *For Christ did not send me to baptize but to preach the Gospel, and not with words of eloquent wisdom, lest the Cross of Christ be emptied of its power. (1 Cor. 1:17)*

And I, when I came to you, brothers, did not come proclaiming to you the testimony of God with lofty speech or wisdom. For I decided to know nothing among you except Jesus Christ and Him crucified. And I was with you in weakness and in fear and much trembling, and my speech and my message were not in plausible words of wisdom, but in demonstration of the Spirit and of power, so that your faith might not rest in the wisdom of men but in the power of God. (1 Cor. 2:1-5)

YOUR TEACHING

TEACH SIMPLY

In Nehemiah 8 we see a beautiful pattern of teaching the Word of God:

> *[Ezra and the Levites] helped the people to understand the Law ... They read from the Book, from the Law of God, clearly, and they gave the sense, so that the people understood the reading. (Neh. 8:8)*[7]

This is how to teach! Simply read the Word of God and then give a straightforward explanation (the sense or meaning) so the people can understand it and obey it.

---

7   Ezra's teaching of the Word came naturally from his own life in the Word. He had set his heart to study the Word, live the Word and obey the Word (Ezra 7:10).

You don't have to be a great scholar. You don't need some "new" unique and exciting revelation. You don't need to find some "deeper" truth in the Bible.

Just read the Word and clarify its meaning, and you will change lives!

> *And all the people went their way to eat and drink and to send portions and to make great rejoicing, because they had understood the words that were declared to them. (Neh. 8:12)*

TEACH THE WORD OF GOD

The Word of God is powerful. It will change lives.

> *For the Word of God is living and active, sharper than any two-edged sword, piercing to the division of soul and of spirit, of joints and of marrow, and discerning the thoughts and intentions of the heart. (Heb. 4:12)*

> *… so shall My Word be that goes out from My mouth; it shall not return to me empty, but it shall accomplish that which I purpose, and shall succeed in the thing for which I sent it. (Is. 55:11)*

> *Is not My Word like fire, declares the Lord, and like a hammer that breaks the rock in pieces? (Jer. 23:29)*

> *It is the Spirit who gives life; the flesh is no help at all. The words that I have spoken to you are Spirit and life. (John 6:63)*
>
> *… Man shall not live by bread alone, but by every Word that comes from the mouth of God. (Matt. 4:4)*
>
> *… Of this you have heard before in the Word of the Truth, the Gospel, which has come to you, as indeed in the whole world it is bearing fruit and increasing – as it also does among you, since the day you heard it and understood the grace of God in truth … (Col. 1:5-6)*
>
> *Like newborn infants, long for the pure spiritual milk, that by it you may grow up into salvation … (1 Pet. 2:2)*

There are so many things we could teach. We could talk about sports, politics, entertainment, the culture, the news, the latest controversies, entertaining stories, research on interesting subjects, human traditions, man's theories, philosophy, psychology, and on and on …

All these things are distractions – they have no power and no authority.

God has called us to primarily focus on teaching the Word of God.

> *Preach the Word; be ready in season and out of season; reprove, rebuke, and exhort, with complete patience and teaching. (2 Tim. 4:2)*

This is why the Early Church was so powerful and had such tremendous impact – because they taught the Word of God! They were not distracted by anything else.

> *Now those who were scattered went about preaching the Word. (Acts 8:4)*

There is no power in anything else. When we teach the Word, we will have authority and we will see lives changed.

> *... Of this you have heard before in the Word of the Truth, the Gospel, which has come to you, as indeed in the whole world it is bearing fruit and increasing – as it also does among you, since the day you heard it and understood the grace of God in truth ... (Col. 3:5-6)*

The Word of God bears fruit and increases – all over the world! In every culture and context, the Word of God will work. It is powerful. All those other things do not work. They are not powerful.

> *And we also thank God constantly for this, that when you received the Word of God, which you heard from us, you accepted it not as the word of men but as what it really is, the Word of God, which is at work in you believers. (1 Thess. 2:13)*

Teach the Word of God and you will build with gold, silver and precious stones (1 Cor. 3:12). All the rest is wood, hay and straw.

Know the Word. Love the Word. Trust the Word. Teach the Word.

Guard your teaching!

DON'T "FILL THE SPACE"

So many times I've heard pastors say, "I was up late on Saturday night, trying to get a message from God to teach on Sunday morning."

Please don't do that! Please stop trying to "get a message" simply to fill the space on Sunday morning.

Don't fill the space. If you don't have a message for the people on Sunday morning, then please don't speak.

Let someone else speak. Perhaps there is someone else who is in touch with God?

Or simply read the Word publicly. That is a biblical and profitable thing to do.

> *Until I come, devote yourself to the public reading of Scripture, to exhortation, to teaching. (1 Tim. 4:13; cf. Col. 4:16; 1 Thess. 5:27; Rev. 1:3)*

That will be so much more powerful than trying to "get a message" simply for the sake of filling the space.

Please stop filling the space!

DON'T SEEK "NEW" REVELATION

Don't seek new revelation. Just teach the clear and simple Word of God. There is so much in the 66 books of the Bible. Most people don't know the Word. They don't need you to come up with weird things.

There is a lot of teaching in churches these days that is pure rubbish.[8] Don't add to the pile.

> *As I urged you when I was going to Macedonia, remain at Ephesus so that you may charge certain persons not to teach any different doctrine, nor to devote themselves to myths and endless genealogies, which*

---

8 Be careful about the Hebrew and Greek "insights" you might hear from other teachers. Such insights are often unsound! Also please do not spiritualize the Scripture. That is very bad biblical interpretation. Teach the clear meaning of the Word.

> *promote speculations rather than the stewardship from God that is by faith. The aim of our charge is love that issues from a pure heart and a good conscience and a sincere faith. Certain persons, by swerving from these, have wandered away into vain discussion, desiring to be teachers of the law, without understanding either what they are saying or the things about which they make confident assertions. (1 Tim. 1:3-7)*

Paul tells Timothy to stop the bad teachers in Ephesus. Their teaching focused on "myths" and other things rather than love, purity and faith. Paul gives many similar exhortations in his letters:

> *Have nothing to do with irreverent, silly myths. Rather train yourself for godliness; (1 Tim. 4:7)*

> *If anyone teaches a different doctrine and does not agree with the sound words of our Lord Jesus Christ and the teaching that accords with godliness, he is puffed up with conceit and understands nothing. He has an unhealthy craving for controversy and for quarrels about words, which produce envy, dissension, slander, evil suspicions, and constant friction among people who are depraved in mind and deprived of the truth, imagining that godliness is a means of gain. (1 Tim. 6:3-5)*

> *O Timothy, guard the deposit entrusted to you. Avoid the irreverent babble and contradictions of what is*

> *falsely called "knowledge," for by professing it some have swerved from the faith … (1 Tim. 6:20-21)*
>
> *Remind them of these things, and charge them before God not to quarrel about words, which does no good, but only ruins the hearers. Do your best to present yourself to God as one approved, a worker who has no need to be ashamed, rightly handling the Word of Truth. But avoid irreverent babble, for it will lead people into more and more ungodliness, and their talk will spread like gangrene … (2 Tim. 2:14-17)*
>
> *Have nothing to do with foolish, ignorant controversies; you know that they breed quarrels. (2 Tim. 2:23)*
>
> *For the time is coming when people will not endure sound teaching, but having itching ears they will accumulate for themselves teachers to suit their own passions, and will turn away from listening to the truth and wander off into myths. (2 Tim. 4:3-4)*

Moreover, avoid teaching the latest exciting trends. There is always some new thing that excites everyone (cf. Acts 17:21).

Guard your teaching. As a teacher you will be judged with "greater strictness":

> *Not many of you should become teachers, my brothers, for you know that we who teach will be judged with greater strictness. (Jam. 3:1)*

Let this bring you a deep fear of God. Teach the clear and simple Word. Then you will build people's lives.

ALWAYS BUILD UP

In Matthew 23, Jesus referred to the teaching of the scribes and Pharisees:

> *The scribes and the Pharisees sit on Moses' seat, so do and observe whatever they tell you, but not the works they do. For they preach, but do not practice. They tie up heavy burdens, hard to bear, and lay them on people's shoulders, but they themselves are not willing to move them with their finger. (Matt. 23:2-4)*

When you're teaching, be careful not to pile up heavy burdens for people. There's a certain kind of teaching that's very easy to do, in which we put together long lists of things that people have to do and not do. We lay these heavy burdens on them and bring them under condemnation. They feel terrible and they may cry and repent, and we think that our teaching has been really effective.

But that is not good teaching. It's easy to create a long list of things that people aren't doing and it makes you look good. But if you'll be honest, you'll admit that you're not doing those things yourself – and you're just like the Pharisees.

This kind of teaching is not helpful. It doesn't build people. It crushes people.

Of course, we need to teach the Truth and follow the Holy Spirit as He brings conviction of sin. But even in the midst of God's fiercest condemnations of man's sin in the Bible, He always gives man hope. He always offers a future. He always offers a clear path of restoration and life.

It's easy to use the Word of God to condemn people, but that's just the law. Instead, draw them to God and to His holiness.

When you teach, you're in the middle of a beautiful interaction between God and His people. God is reaching out to His people. His people are turning toward Him.

Do everything to build up God's people. Even when you're sharing something negative or corrective or convicting, it must always be done with love and care, and it must always be to build up.

But the wisdom from above is first pure, then peaceable, gentle, open to reason, full of mercy and good fruits, impartial and sincere. (Jam. 3:17)

RESPECT THE PRIVILEGE OF TEACHING

Sometimes teachers take advantage of their opportunity in addressing a group of people to hit back at certain people who have criticized or wronged them in the past. This is a great abuse.

Teaching must never be used to punish or attack people. Instead you must embrace the Cross, die to your own feelings of hurt and resist this temptation of fighting back.

Your purpose must always be to build.

> ... *Let all things be done for building up. (1 Cor. 14:26)*

Of course, sometimes that will involve correction. At those times, you must be very honest before God in your own heart. What is your motivation for correcting? Are you just punishing people? Are you trying to get them back for something? Or is there really a redemptive purpose in the correction?[9]

If there is any doubt in your heart about your own motive, then you should not do it. You should not bring the correction. If there is a bit of anger, hurt or unforgiveness towards the people, then you shouldn't do it.

God has given you the responsibility to bless, to heal, to build up. If you correct, then let it be truly from love.

A true teacher has considerable authority and power in his words. Consequently, if you have a strong teaching gift and authority and you use that to express your own unforgiveness and anger, you will damage people.

> *For this reason I write these things while I am away from you, that when I come I may not have to be severe in my use of the authority that the Lord has given me for building up and not for tearing down. (2 Cor. 13:10)*

Paul speaks about the authority that God gave him to build up, not to tear down.

---

[9] Don't rebuke people who fall asleep during your teaching. The fact that they fall asleep could mean several things. Perhaps they simply need sleep. Perhaps you're boring. Perhaps you've gone too long like Paul in Acts 20:19. In any case, it's not appropriate to humiliate them. Just let them sleep – apparently, they need it!

It's true that Paul did a lot of correction, but he did it with weeping; he did it with love and he did it to build.

> *Therefore be alert, remembering that for three years I did not cease night or day to admonish every one with tears. (Acts 20:31)*

> *For I wrote to you out of much affliction and anguish of heart and with many tears, not to cause you pain but to let you know the abundant love that I have for you. (2 Cor. 2:4)*

> *For many, of whom I have often told you and now tell you even with tears, walk as enemies of the Cross of Christ. (Phil. 3:18)*

Please be honest with yourself. The more faithful you are and the purer you are, the more authority God will give you – He will give you a higher level of grace, a greater level of gifting. If you're faithful with a little, He'll give you more (Matt. 25:23). But if you use the gifting and the authority He's given you to express your own frustration and hurt, that is a deep abuse of the gifting of God.

This is one reason why many leaders remain at a low level of authority and influence. If they had more power, they'd be calling fire down from heaven to destroy all their detractors!

You must be pure. If you're pure with a little bit of gifting from God, He'll give you more.

So, don't ask God for more authority and for more influence. Instead, ask Him for purity. As you are pure with a little, He'll give you more.

THE LIMITS OF THE TEACHER

There are three major limits every teacher should recognize.

First is the limit of what the people can actually handle. You should be aware of this and respect it.

> *I still have many things to say to you, but you cannot bear them now. When the Spirit of Truth comes, He will guide you into all the truth … (John 16:12-13)*

Jesus deliberately limited His teaching to what He knew His disciples could handle, while entrusting them to the ongoing help of the Holy Spirit who would take them into full maturity.

Your goal as a teacher is not to try to make everyone perfect in one big jump. Your goal is to help them take a step in the right direction.

In addition, please remember that not everyone will yield a "hundredfold" return. Some will yield sixty, and some thirty (Matt. 13:8). Be a gentle shepherd who helps the people to take the small steps that are right for them at this time. Don't worry about how their fruitfulness makes you look – your purpose is to serve them, not yourself. What do they need right now and what are they capable of?

Second is the limit of your own relationship with those you're teaching. How much favor do you have with them? How much do they know you? How much do they trust you?

For those with whom you have a very deep relationship you can speak more freely than with people who are "new" to you or who are outside your normal circles of influence.

Paul recognized that he had God-ordained "areas of influence."

> *But we will not boast beyond limits, but will boast only with regard to the area of influence God assigned to us, to reach even to you. (2 Cor. 10:13)*

Consequently, if he, or one of his spiritual sons, had planted the church, then he was very free within that church and he took a high level of initiative and responsibility in any area he thought necessary. Outside of those circles of influence he would have been more limited.

Favor with people is earned. It cannot simply be demanded. And with favor comes the freedom to go deeper.

When you go to a new group, ask them, "What do you want? What is most helpful for me to teach on?" They may answer, "Whatever the Lord leads you," but you've come in as a servant, not as a lord. When you do that, you will earn favor and people will trust you. You will have proven that you really care for them and that you're not trying to use them. When you're not harsh or demanding, and when you're not trying to correct everything, then they will grow to trust you, and they will welcome you more and more deeply. Eventually you'll get to the place where they may ask you to deal with difficult, complicated things. That will happen because you have earned favor – you have served them, you've been gentle. You have proven that you really love them, and that they can trust you.

In particular, you should *never* deal with controversial subjects in a group that is not "your own" unless you are very specifically asked to address it.

Third is the limit of your own gifting and capacity.

> *For by the grace given to me I say to everyone among you not to think of himself more highly than he ought to think, but to think with sober judgment, each according to the measure of faith that God has assigned.*

> *For as in one body we have many members, and the members do not all have the same function, so we, though many, are one body in Christ, and individually members one of another.*

> *Having gifts that differ according to the grace given to us, let us use them: if prophecy, in proportion to our faith; if service, in our serving; the one who teaches, in his teaching; the one who exhorts, in his exhortation; the one who contributes, in generosity; the one who leads, with zeal; the one who does acts of mercy, with cheerfulness. (Rom. 12:3-8)*

In Romans 12, Paul teaches that we have different gifts and different measures, or depths, of those giftings (v. 3 "each according to the measure of faith that God has assigned"; cf. Eph. 4:7), and that we should function in our gifts according to that "proportion" (v. 6).

Just because you're a teacher doesn't mean you can teach on everything! A lot of damage has been done by teachers who taught outside their areas of expertise and experience, or, for example, by evangelists who were so gifted in evangelism that they assumed they were therefore able to teach deep doctrine.

We should recognize the current limits of our own knowledge and ability as teachers and stay within those limits. It may be tempting to always have an answer for every question or to teach on any and every subject, but that is not appropriate for any of us.

> *… I say to everyone among you not to think of himself more highly than he ought to think, but to think with sober judgment, each according to the measure of faith that God has assigned. (Rom. 12:3)*

TEACHING AND EXHORTATION

Not everyone who speaks in the church is called to be a "teacher." In reality, many are called to be "exhorters."

In Romans 12:7-8, Paul distinguishes between these two gifts:

> ... *the one who teaches, in his teaching; the one who exhorts, in his exhortation* ...

They are both God-given and they are both extremely valuable, but they are different.

Of course, a leader can have both gifts. Paul had both. In his letters and speaking he integrated them both with great effect.

The fact is that many frontline leaders in churches around the world are called to be exhorters and not teachers.

Exhortation is vital. The church needs exhortation to build us up, to encourage us, and, at times, to warn us. There are examples of this in Acts:

> *The report of this [many people in Antioch turning to Christ] came to the ears of the church in Jerusalem, and they sent Barnabas to Antioch. When he came and saw the grace of God, he was glad, and he exhorted them all to remain faithful to the Lord with steadfast purpose, for he was a good man, full of the Holy Spirit and of faith. And a great many people were added to the Lord. (Acts 11:22-24)*

> *And Judas and Silas, who were themselves prophets, encouraged and strengthened the brothers with many words. (Acts 15:32)*

Sadly, many local church leaders who are gifted in exhortation are under pressure to teach. Consequently, they try to come up with deep teachings to fulfill everyone's expectations. However, since they're not gifted in that area their teaching is, at best, weak or, at worst, erroneous. What they should do is *exhort* the people: encouraging them, building them up, comforting them, warning them.

Exhortation is a tremendous ministry. It builds the church. We need exhorters. Consequently, we should not put pressure on everyone to have to teach. This will spare the church a great deal of confusion.

Moreover, we need to make a good place for exhorters in the church because we need them.

> *Until I come, devote yourself to the public reading of Scripture, to exhortation, to teaching. (1 Tim. 4:13)*

When we only recognize the teaching ministry as valuable then many exhorters try to teach and fail. In addition, we are robbed of the exhortation they should be giving. When you're discouraged, for example, you may not need a teacher. You probably need an exhorter.

We should honor each member of the Body in their own proper place doing what they do well to God's glory.

PREPARE YOUR HEART, NOT JUST YOUR HEAD

A dear friend said to me, "When I'm called upon to teach spontaneously, I can do it really well. I teach freely and naturally, and it leads people into God's presence. It's life giving. But if I am required to prepare, then it's hard for me. And the results are not as good."

This appears counterintuitive. One would expect that with more time to prepare the quality should be higher. But let's look more deeply at this.

When you are suddenly called upon to teach a group of people, then you have no opportunity to prepare and no opportunity to start figuring things out for yourself, so you are more likely to depend on God and not on yourself and your own preparation.

As you look at God, turning your heart to Him, listening to Him, depending on Him, He will speak to you (e.g., Luke 12:11-12). Then as you respond out of what He gives you, it will be a beautiful flow of life.

But when you have time to prepare, you might start trying to figure it out. It's very easy to trust in your own knowledge and to make your own plans about what you should and shouldn't teach. As a result, your teaching contains a lot of your knowledge, energy and vision.

This does not mean that it's wrong to prepare! On the contrary. You must diligently prepare, but make sure that it's the right *kind* of preparation.

When you're preparing to teach, your primary preparation should be a preparation of heart, not just of head. In your preparation, bring your heart before God and, in His Presence, empty out your own motives, agendas and purposes and your trust in your own knowledge.

This is a big shift of thinking for almost everyone who is involved in teaching because usually, teachers do a preparation of head and not of heart. And then when they're teaching they wonder why, although the content is good and accurate biblical truth, it just doesn't go anywhere – there's no life to it.

What they should be doing instead is preparation of heart, bringing their hearts before God in a place of submission, surrender and dependency, looking at God as they look at the Word and are reflecting on what they're going to teach.

Bring the Word before God, pray over it, pray over the people you're about to teach, asking God to use you to help them, asking God to give you His direction, His burden, His life. Wait upon Him with dependency and trust. He will give you life. This is the preparation of the heart.

As we will see in the next section, throughout your life, you should be spending a great deal of time in the Word – learning the Word, growing in the Word. Then when you prepare for a specific teaching, you'll have not only solid content and sound biblical interpretation, but you'll also have life.

A LIFESTYLE OF PREPARATION IN THE WORD OF GOD

Your foundation for teaching must be your lifestyle of being in Word of God. This means that you are continually studying the Word simply because you love God and want to know Him. It is not so that you can give a teaching to others.

Then, as you're reading the Scripture, if you're not sure about what something means you may check out some commentaries, and look at the cultural and historical context, and get into the original languages. This involves a rich, intellectual engagement with the Scriptures as well as a deep, spiritual one. Over time, you will thoroughly learn the Word. But the purpose of this study is to build your life, not to give a teaching. This is an important distinction.

This lifestyle will provide for you a deep well from which you can draw for a specific teaching. So then when you're preparing for a particular teaching time, you will not be trying to learn a big body of information and put it all together in a presentation, but instead you'll be asking God, "Lord, what are you saying to this people right now?" Your existing knowledge of the Word will be the well from which you draw.

We see Ezra's preparation in the Word:

> *For Ezra had set his heart to study the Law of the Lord, and to do it and to teach His statutes and rules in Israel. (Ezra 7:10)*

Ezra set his heart to study the Word and obey the Word. Then his teaching (for example, in Nehemiah 8:8) came naturally from his own life in the Word.

If you do this, you will find that your teaching will move to a much higher level. It will have a deeper engagement with the people. There will be a greater spiritual authority on your teaching. There will be greater spiritual substance in your teaching. And there will be greater spiritual fruit that will come from it.

When teachers' engagement with the Word is only when they have to give a certain teaching, then their preparation will be largely informational. Consequently, when they teach, they will be under pressure to cover the content and cram all the information in. They will be heavily invested in the information they prepared and not so much in the spiritual purpose of God for the teaching. As a result, it will not be very effective in bringing life change.

AVOID THE TWO EXTREMES

Regarding preparation, these are the two extremes to avoid:

- Great preparation and planning and then following your plan rigidly and meticulously with no room for the Holy Spirit to do anything.
- No preparation or planning under the guise of being led by the Holy Spirit.

Here is how to avoid these extremes. First, spend a lot of time in the Word of God. Be in the Word because you love God and you want to know Him and serve Him.

It's fine to also spend some time in other books but your primary focus should be the Bible itself. The Word of God is alive. It will change you!

> *... The words that I have spoken to you are Spirit and life. (John 6:63)*
>
> *... the living and enduring Word of God. (1 Pet. 1:23)*

As you're in the Word, learn the principles of sound biblical interpretation[10] and also use the various tools to go deeply into the Scripture – in particular the language tools.

This time you spend in the Word will be the foundation for all of your teaching ministry.

When you need to give a specific teaching, let your primary preparation be that of the heart, as well as intercession for the people you're about to teach, as described in the previous sections.

Then when you are teaching, be led by the Holy Spirit. He knows the real needs of the people and how to address those needs.

Here is the balance. You should work hard on preparation. Do not use the idea of "I'm going to be led by the Holy Spirit" as an excuse for laziness. If you follow that path, then you will torture the people with shallow, repetitious, self-indulgent nonsense. Such teachers mistake whatever pops into their head for the voice of God. Sometimes, they merely repeat the last conversation they had with someone since it's fresh in their minds!

---

10 For example, see *What Does the Bible Say?* by Malcolm Webber.

Jesus spent a great deal of time in preparation. He spent hours and hours with His Father. If He needed to prepare, how much more do you?

Prepare deeply in the Word and in your heart. Know what you're going to teach. But then, when you are teaching, hold what you have prepared in an open hand. Don't be limited by what you have prepared. And don't be under pressure to have to "cover" it all. Follow the Holy Spirit as He guides you.

Often in church, we pray, "Lord, please have Your way!" and then we go on methodically following our own predetermined plans.

Be led by the Spirit but don't use that as an excuse for laziness. Work hard at preparation, yield to the Holy Spirit, and you will do well.

TEACH WHAT YOU KNOW IS REAL

Teach what's alive to you and comes out of your life. Teach reality – not theory or someone else's experience. Prove it and then teach it. Then you can share your own stories and not someone else's.

If it changed your life, it will probably change others' lives! So, focus on what's life to you.

It's hard for many people to teach because they don't engage God very deeply in their own life. As a result, when they try to teach the Word, they're just talking theory.

If you are to teach well, you must first find God for yourself in His Word and in your life. Then, out of that you can teach others. Only then will your teaching be life.

When reading the Bible, we need to think about who the author was and what he experienced. What made him write what he wrote? The authors of the Bible wrote out of their life experiences. They did not teach mere theory. They experienced God. Truth was revealed and taught through their lives, not just on paper in their writings.

This means it's very costly to be a teacher. You have to experience life very deeply; otherwise, you won't find God in a deep way. Effective teaching is not simply the result of having a teaching gift or a lot of knowledge. It comes from having a deep life in God.

Don't look for teachings. Look for God, for life, for truth, for His dealings in your own life. Then you will have plenty of teachings for others whenever you need them. And then your writing and teaching will transform lives – it will never be mere theory! If it has first changed your life, it will have deep life-changing power in it. You will be passionate about it.[11] And it will change your readers and hearers.

Finally, don't teach on subjects or passages that are not clear to you. Certainly, there are some parts of the Bible that are harder to understand than others (2 Pet. 3:16).[12] But there is much that is plain. Teach what is clear and your teaching will carry weight and authority.

---

11 Over the years, I've been asked many times, "How can you be so passionate when you teach?" My response is, "Really? I didn't notice I was passionate. I'm not trying to be passionate. I just believe what I teach!"

12 In your teaching you should focus mostly on "Level 1" matters as well as some "Level 2." You should avoid "Level 3." Please see *The Three Levels of Authority of Doctrine and Practice* by Malcolm Webber for more on this distinction.

TEACH SOUNDLY

Work hard to be a skilled teacher of the Word.

Learn the basic principles of biblical interpretation. These days there is a vast amount of help available.[13] Don't be lazy.

> *Do your best to present yourself to God as one approved, a worker who has no need to be ashamed, rightly handling the Word of Truth. (2 Tim. 2:15)*

---

13 For example, see *What Does the Bible Say?* by Malcolm Webber.

DON'T IMITATE THE ACADEMICS

In 2 Corinthians 10, Paul quotes the criticisms of his detractors:

> *For they say, "His letters are weighty and strong, but his bodily presence is weak, and his speech of no account."*
> *(2 Cor. 10:10)*

It's unlikely that Paul was a boring speaker.

> *… our Gospel came to you not only in word, but also in power and in the Holy Spirit and with full conviction.*
> *(1 Thess. 1:5)*

But, apparently, he was not that polished when compared to others of his day.

> *Even if I am unskilled in speaking, I am not so in knowledge; indeed, in every way we have made this plain to you in all things. (2 Cor. 11:6)*

Paul acknowledged he was not a trained speaker. But that didn't bother him.

Consider the context of these words. Corinth was in Greece and the Greeks of Paul's day pursued knowledge and had a high respect for oratory. They highly regarded those who could speak impressively. That was Greek culture.

Paul didn't have the same skills that the Greek scholars had. The scholars had complicated abstract knowledge and they had an accomplished and polished way of speaking. Consequently, when the false teachers looked at Paul, they held him in contempt for his lack of "professional" speaking ability.

Paul acknowledged that he was not skilled but also that he was not trying to be. He was not competing with the academics and the scholars. He was not competing with the great polished speakers. He was not interested in any of that. In fact, he considered that sort of thing "dung" (Phil. 3:8).

Instead, Paul taught out of life. He had found the Lord Jesus. He was walking with God. He was depending on God. He was looking at God. He loved the Word. The Word by the Spirit had changed his life. And out of this inward reality he taught. He was not following some outward, polished, mechanical form. He was not competing with the scholars and orators. He taught the Truth in the power of the Spirit!

> *And I, when I came to you, brothers, did not come proclaiming to you the testimony of God with lofty speech or wisdom. For I decided to know nothing among you except Jesus Christ and Him crucified. And I was with you in weakness and in fear and much trembling, and my speech and my message were not in plausible words of wisdom, but in demonstration of the Spirit and of power, so that your faith might not rest in the wisdom of men but in the power of God. (1 Cor. 2:1-5)*

WAIT ON GOD WHILE YOU TEACH

When Jesus taught, He continually looked at His Father, waiting upon Him.

> ... the Son can do nothing of His own accord, but only what He sees the Father doing. For whatever the Father does, that the Son does likewise. For the Father loves the Son and shows Him all that He Himself is doing ... (John 5:19-20)

We see this dramatically in John 8. The scribes and Pharisees brought the woman caught in adultery and asked Jesus whether they should stone her. It was a brilliant question designed to trick Him. If He said, "No, don't stone her, but show her mercy" then He would be contradicting the Law of Moses. But if he said, "Yes, do stone her as the law commands," He would be contradicting His own teaching on the grace and forgiveness of God. In response, Jesus "bent down and wrote with His finger on the ground" (v. 6).

There are many views about what it was that Jesus wrote on the ground, but is that really the point? It's possible He was simply pausing to inwardly look at His Father, loving Him, listening to Him. Then out of that inward divine wisdom He spoke so incredibly: "Let him who is without sin among you be the first to throw a stone at her" (v. 7), putting them all to shame and to silence.

You should teach the same way, by the Spirit, continually looking at God. Don't be in a hurry to teach or to respond to hard questions. Pause when necessary. Write on the ground. Listen to God. Don't rely on your own knowledge and experience. Look at God. Depend on Him. He will speak to you if you wait on Him.

The New Testament teaches that the Holy Spirit will speak to you:

> *But the Counselor, the Holy Spirit, whom the Father will send in My name, will teach you all things and will remind you of everything I have said to you. (John 14:26)*

> *But when He, the Spirit of Truth, comes, He will guide you into all truth. He will not speak on His own; He will speak only what He hears, and He will tell you what is yet to come. He will bring glory to Me by taking from what is Mine and making it known to you. All that belongs to the Father is Mine. That is why I said*

> *the Spirit will take from what is Mine and make it known to you. (John 16:13-15)*
>
> *Now we have received not the spirit of the world, but the Spirit who is from God, that we might understand the things freely given us by God. And we impart this in words not taught by human wisdom but taught by the Spirit, interpreting spiritual truths to those who are spiritual. (1 Cor. 1:12-13)*

Especially at the beginning of your teaching, don't just launch into what you've prepared. Pause. Look at God. Wait on God. You might be surprised by what happens.

> *The wind blows where it wishes, and you hear its sound, but you do not know where it comes from or where it goes. So it is with everyone who is born of the Spirit. (John 3:8)*

In John 3, Jesus gave a beautiful metaphor for the life and ministry of every believer and it's especially true for teachers.

He said, "You hear its sound, but you do not know where it comes from or where it goes." You can tell that the wind is blowing. You can hear the wind. You can feel the wind. You can see its results. But you don't know why it's blowing, and you don't know where it came from or where it's going next.

It's the same when you're teaching. You can tell what the Holy Spirit is doing. You can hear it. You can see it. But you don't necessarily know why. You don't necessarily know what will happen next. But you don't have to! You must depend on the Holy Spirit. It's His work.

Jesus said, "The wind blows where it wishes." You can't control the wind. Have you ever tried? It's the same with the Holy Spirit. You can't control Him with your plan. He will do whatever He wants.

Therefore, you must depend on Him and continually look at Him, loving Him, listening to Him and following Him. This is how to teach.

The Holy Spirit knows the people – their needs and struggles. And He will use you to help them. Therefore, depend on Him to lead you. This is true "co-laboring" with God.

> *For we are God's fellow workers. You are God's field, God's building. (1 Cor. 3:9)*

This may be a little scary when you first try to do it. But the more you do this, the more comfortable you'll become. He will never let you down.

Of course, you'll never do this perfectly, but the more you work with God, and the more you teach this way, the better at it you'll be. You'll become more and more confident to trust God and to follow His direction rather than rigidly staying with your own preparation. You will experience a higher level of authority in your teaching. You will experience a deeper impact in the lives of those you're serving. And it will be the right kind of impact – His life, union with Him.

When you see the results of teaching this way, you'll decide that this is the only way to teach!

WATCH GOD AND WATCH THE PEOPLE

There are two directions you should always look while you teach.

As we just saw, you must always wait on God, looking at Him, listening to Him, surrendered to Him. He knows perfectly what the people need.

But you must also look at the people. How are they responding? Do they understand what you're teaching? Do they agree? Disagree? Are they excited? Are they convicted? If they're convicted, then stop and pray. Have them pray. Don't just continue on.

Watch God and the people and respond to them both.

DON'T BE AFRAID

Don't be disturbed by the faces of those you're teaching.

People can look angry when they're being convicted or are listening intently.

Also, people can look bored and disengaged when they're actually listening closely and being deeply impacted.

Trust God. His Word is alive, and it will do the work.

> *For as the rain and the snow come down from heaven and do not return there but water the earth, making it bring forth and sprout, giving seed to the sower and bread to the eater, so shall My Word be that goes out from My mouth; it shall not return to Me empty, but*

it shall accomplish that which I purpose, and shall succeed in the thing for which I sent it. (Is. 55:10-11)

USE THE "FOUR DYNAMICS" WHEN YOU TEACH

Deep change occurs in a person's life through the "Four Dynamics of Transformation" (the "4Ds"):[14]

- Spiritual Dynamics – including prayer, worship, reflection, meditation in the Word;
- Relational Dynamics – including encouragement, accountability, examples, mentors, coaches;
- Experiential Dynamics – including obedience, learning by doing, challenging assignments, and pressure;
- Instructional Dynamics – the teaching of the Word of God in an engaging and interactive way, integrating

---

14 Please see the LeaderSource course *Building Healthy Leaders*.

doctrine into the context of life, experiences and relationships.

In a long-term training program, it's straightforward to harness all four. But even if you've only got an hour or less to teach, you still can use all four dynamics.

At a bare minimum you can teach the Word (Instructional) in the Presence of the Holy Spirit (Spiritual), share your life (Relational), and call the people to specific action (Experiential).

Thus, you should *always* use the "Four Dynamics" when you teach.

ALWAYS TEACH WITH CLARITY, PASSION AND CREDIBILITY

There are three characteristics of effective communication of any kind: clarity, passion and credibility.

First, your teaching must be *clear*. As we said previously, teaching is an act of leadership and leadership means movement. Before the people can begin to move, they must first understand the direction they are going. Therefore, your teaching must be clear.

> *But we have renounced disgraceful, underhanded ways. We refuse to practice cunning or to tamper with God's Word, but by the open statement of the truth we would commend ourselves to everyone's conscience in the sight of God. (2 Cor. 4:2)*

> *Even if I am unskilled in speaking, I am not so in knowledge; indeed, in every way we have made this plain to you in all things. (2 Cor. 11:6)*
>
> *At the same time, pray also for us, that God may open to us a door for the Word, to declare the mystery of Christ, on account of which I am in prison – that I may make it clear, which is how I ought to speak. (Col. 4:3-4)*

Consequently, do not obscure your teaching with big words, complicated thoughts and abstract theories. Make the Word of God plain! Let every word have weight.

> *… Write the vision; make it plain on tablets, so he may run who reads it. (Hab. 2:2)*
>
> *And if the bugle gives an indistinct sound, who will get ready for battle? (1 Cor. 14:8)*

Second, your teaching must be *passionate*. Change almost always involves a cost of some kind. Sometimes it involves a lot of pain! If you're not passionate about what you're saying, you should not expect your hearers to be passionate about it and to be willing to pay the price of change. Therefore, your teaching must be passionate – not simply an expression of emotions, but an expression of the intensity of your own passion for what you're saying. If you don't passionately believe it, you should not expect others to!

> So, being affectionately desirous of you, we were ready to share with you not only the Gospel of God but also our own selves, because you had become very dear to us. (1 Thess. 2:8)

Accordingly, express your love and affection both for the Truth and for the people you serve. Let your passion out!

> If I say, "I will not mention Him, or speak anymore in His Name," there is in my heart as it were a burning fire shut up in my bones, and I am weary with holding it in, and I cannot. (Jer. 20:9)

> … we cannot but speak of what we have seen and heard. (Acts 4:20)

> … for three years I did not cease night or day to admonish everyone with tears. (Acts 20:31)

> For I wrote to you out of much affliction and anguish of heart and with many tears, not to cause you pain but to let you know the abundant love that I have for you. (2 Cor. 2:4)

> For God is my witness, how I yearn for you all with the affection of Christ Jesus. (Phil. 1:8)

> For you know how, like a father with his children, we exhorted each one of you and encouraged you and

> *charged you to walk in a manner worthy of God, who calls you into His own Kingdom and glory. (1 Thess. 2:11-12)*

Third, your teaching must be *credible*. If you're asking others to follow you, they must trust you.

Therefore, the life of the teacher must be beyond reproach.

> *For our boast is this, the testimony of our conscience, that we behaved in the world with simplicity and godly sincerity, not by earthly wisdom but by the grace of God, and supremely so toward you. (2 Cor. 1:12)*
>
> *We put no obstacle in anyone's way, so that no fault may be found with our ministry, but as servants of God we commend ourselves in every way ... (2 Cor. 6:3-4)*
>
> *... You know what kind of men we proved to be among you for your sake. (1 Thess. 1:5)*
>
> *You are witnesses, and God also, how holy and righteous and blameless was our conduct toward you believers. (1 Thess. 2:10)*
>
> *Command and teach these things. Let no one despise you for your youth, but set the believers an example in speech, in conduct, in love, in faith, in purity. (1 Tim. 4:11-12)*

> *Show yourself in all respects to be a model of good works, and in your teaching show integrity, dignity, and sound speech that cannot be condemned, so that an opponent may be put to shame, having nothing evil to say about us. (Tit. 2:7-8)*

> *… in your hearts honor Christ the Lord as holy, always being prepared to make a defense to anyone who asks you for a reason for the hope that is in you; yet do it with gentleness and respect, having a good conscience, so that, when you are slandered, those who revile your good behavior in Christ may be put to shame. (1 Pet. 3:15-16)*

In addition, when you teach, be respectful toward everyone – both in your words and in your body language. Earn their trust.

Every time you teach, your teaching must have all three characteristics: clarity, passion and credibility.[15]

---

15 This is true for communication of every kind. If it has all three characteristics, it will be far more effective.

HAVE ONE POINT

When you only have a short time to teach, make sure you have only one point – one point around which everything revolves.

If you try to say too much, none of it will be effective. Notice in the Gospels how focused Jesus' teaching was.

Have one point and make it well.

If you can change somebody's life in a single area or change one attitude or correct one error or misunderstanding, or if you have helped him to establish one new behavior, you've done a great job!

Don't be a perfectionist. Don't drive the people. Be patient with them just as God has been patient with you. Don't insist that they all produce a hundredfold return (Mark 4:20). For many, the best they will ever do is thirtyfold and some even less.

Your goal for the people you're teaching is to help them take one step.

That's realistic. They can take one step. Not many people can take more than that.

This requires that you have a clear grasp of what that step should be. As you prepare to teach, ask God what the step should be. When you are clear about this, your teaching will be effective.

DIALOGUE WITH THE PEOPLE YOU'RE TEACHING

Throughout your teaching, you need to interact with those you're teaching.

We see this in Jesus' teaching ministry. He was constantly asking questions and going back and forth with those He taught. It was not just one-way.

There are numerous reasons for this:

- People learn through their own discovery and not just being told. The effective teacher will lead them through this process of discovery.
- You may think you've taught one thing, while in reality the people heard something else completely different. You

will only discover this if you give them the chance to tell you.
- People learn when they are engaged, not when they're passive and bored.
- You don't know it all. When the people interact, they will contribute meaningful things that become integrated into the rich teaching experience for everyone.
- The Holy Spirit is not only speaking to you. He's speaking to others as well. If you listen carefully you will hear His voice through others. Together we have the fullness of God (Eph. 3:19). Together we can hear His voice so much more deeply.

What then, brothers? When you come together, each one has a hymn, a lesson, a revelation, a tongue, or an interpretation. Let all things be done for building up. (1 Cor. 14:26)

This does not lessen your authority as a teacher at all. In fact, it establishes you as a healthy teacher who recognizes your dependence on the rest of the Body of Christ.

ASK GOOD QUESTIONS

Effective teaching is not just in having the right answers but also in asking good questions.

Jesus constantly asked questions as He taught. For example, in Matthew 16:13-18, His question, "Who do people say that the Son of Man is?" led to Peter's profound insight, "You are the Christ, the Son of the living God." This revelation was so great that Jesus said He would build His Church on it!

A good question requires people to think. This encourages them to take responsibility for their own learning.

A good question is not a "closed question" – the answer cannot simply be "yes" or "no."

Moreover, a good question is not simply "fishing" for the right answer (although this does have its place to ensure people are learning the right things). When you ask questions, genuinely be curious about what people will have to share. Sometimes some profound insights will come out – far beyond what you had intended to teach.

Neither should a question be a childish one. For example, if a teacher says, "Jesus died on the Cross for our sins … Why did Jesus die on the Cross?" (expected answer: "For our sins"), he is not treating people as adults but as children.

When asking questions, it's a good idea to have some quality answers in the back of your mind in advance. If you can't answer your own question, how can anyone else? If necessary, you can provide one answer to give an example. You can also keep the dialogue going until all your answers have been mentioned by others.

Asking good questions takes practice to do well. Begin doing so today!

TAKE EVERY OPPORTUNITY TO PRACTICE

No one taught perfectly on their first occasion.

You will learn by doing.

Don't wait until you have perfect knowledge of the Scriptures and are able to perfectly hear the voice of the Holy Spirit in every situation. You will be waiting a long time for this!

Of course, do limit your content to what you're sure about. Don't act like an expert in areas in which you are weak. But take advantage of every opportunity.

Teach in small groups,[16] teach in large groups, teach anywhere at any time. Teach when you're prepared. Teach when you're not prepared.

The more you teach, the better at it you will become.

---

16 The author began his teaching ministry more than 40 years ago by teaching two people each week. Be faithful in a little and God will give you more.

SOME PRACTICAL ADVICE

- Never violate confidentiality. Someone may have privately shared something with you that you'd love to mention in a teaching to illustrate a point – don't!
- Don't talk about your family unless you ask them first.
- Don't say "in closing" unless you really are closing. There is nothing more irritating than repeated "in closings"!
- Be very careful with humor – especially in cross-cultural contexts. What is funny in one culture will frequently not be funny in other cultures and may even be offensive. This is especially true of teasing. Often, it's good to avoid joking altogether – it's simply too risky – especially when you don't know the people. Remember that in some cultures, people often laugh when embarrassed, not amused.

- Be conscious of your body language. If you stand too casually it can express either arrogance or insecurity. Watch your hands and feet.
- Be respectful to those you teach (1 Tim. 5:1-2).
- Smile often when you teach!
- If you're asked a question and don't know the answer, don't make it up. Acknowledge you don't know and commit to getting back to them when you've had time to look into it.
- Listen to your audio recordings and watch your video recordings. Do both – that way you'll listen carefully to how you use your voice and the words you use, and you'll also watch your own body language. Be your own critic. This may be unpleasant for you but there's no better way to improve!
- Only talk about yourself if it genuinely illustrates a point (e.g., 2 Cor. 1:8-11) and points people to Christ. "Sir we would like to see Jesus!" (John 12:21)
- Keep a record of what you teach – when, where and to whom. This may save you the embarrassment of repeating the same teaching.
- When someone offers you a breath mint, take it. Apparently, you need it.
- When teaching over a several-day period, change your clothes each day. Remember that the people have to look at you! Having two changes of clothing can be sufficient if you mix up the components.
- Pray constantly about your teaching – before, during and after.

PROTECT YOUR LIFE

Watch your life and doctrine closely. Persevere in them, because if you do, you will save both yourself and your hearers. (1 Tim. 4:16)

Paul tells you to protect your life and your teaching closely. In fact, your eternal salvation depends on it.

Notice which comes first – your life.

Growing in capacity to teach is not just through studying books about the Bible. The depth of your capacity to teach is the direct result of the depth of your union with Christ, your character, and the servanthood of your life.

The life of the teacher must be one that is continually growing in Christ.

Teaching the Word when your own spiritual life is weak is hard to do. This is why many Christian teachers and preachers are weary. Sometimes they give up altogether.

We can do a lot of good things in our own strength for a while. Some people are more disciplined than others and can go for a long time. But eventually it becomes very dry.

Significantly, it is possible for others to be genuinely blessed by what you teach even though you are not walking with God yourself (Phil. 1:15-18). The content of your teaching may be biblically sound so people can be helped. But it won't benefit you if you're not walking with Him.

You must closely guard your life. No one else will do this for you!

Paul guarded his life:

> *Do you not know that in a race all the runners run, but only one receives the prize? So run that you may obtain it. Every athlete exercises self-control in all things. They do it to receive a perishable wreath, but we an imperishable. So I do not run aimlessly; I do not box as one beating the air. But I discipline my body and keep it under control, lest after preaching to others I myself should be disqualified. (1 Cor. 9:24-27)*

On the Last Day, God is not going to be impressed with us – even though we may have a lot of outward ministry fruitfulness – if our lives have not been lived in purity and the fear of God. God looks for the image of His Son in our lives.

ABOVE ALL THINGS, LIVE IN UNION WITH CHRIST

God is calling you to teach others out of your own inward life.

> *... apart from Me you can do nothing. (John 15:5)*

You have been invited to participate in the great eternal fellowship of love and life in the Godhead. That is your invitation. If you look at Him, you will have strength. You will bear fruit that pleases Him. You won't simply produce wood, hay and straw that is burned on the Last Day.

You have only one life. Don't waste it but pursue the very highest purpose. He is your highest purpose. This is the true nature of spiritual ministry and of teaching.

As God has called you and given you the privilege of teaching His Word, live out of His life. Teach out of His life. Then you will do well, and the people you serve will do well. Lives will be changed, and Jesus will live more and more wonderfully in His Church. The precious Bride of Christ will be nurtured. The Church will not be just a religious machine, but she will be the beautiful Bride of Christ – the spotless Bride eagerly waiting for His return.

FINAL WORDS

If there are only two things that you do in your teaching ministry, let those two things be these:

1. Do everything out of union with Christ. Throughout your life, be in the Word to know Him. Before you teach, prepare your heart before Him. While you teach, look at Him, depend on Him, listen to Him.
2. When you teach, read the Word and give the sense.

And you will do well!

May God raise you up as a new kind of teacher in your nation – with a heart of servanthood, love and gentleness.

May you teach by the power of the Spirit of God, not just from human wisdom and techniques. May you teach with deep authority, conviction, and clear Truth.

May your words not tickle people's ears but deeply change their hearts and lives. May God let none of your words fall to the ground.

May God give you a greater hunger for His Word so that you won't only go to His Word when you need to teach something, but that every day you will feed upon His Word, dig deeply in His Word, and find life! Then, from the depth of that life, you will have life for others. Then leaders and disciples will be built, and healthy churches will be raised up. And the glory of God will be revealed across your nation and from there to the rest of the world.

Strategic Press
www.StrategicPress.org

Strategic Press is a division of Strategic Global Assistance, Inc.
www.sgai.org

513 S. Main St. Suite 2
Elkhart, IN 46516
U.S.A

+1-844-532-3371 (LEADER-1)

www.ingramcontent.com/pod-product-compliance
Lightning Source LLC
LaVergne TN
LVHW051837080426
835512LV00018B/2929